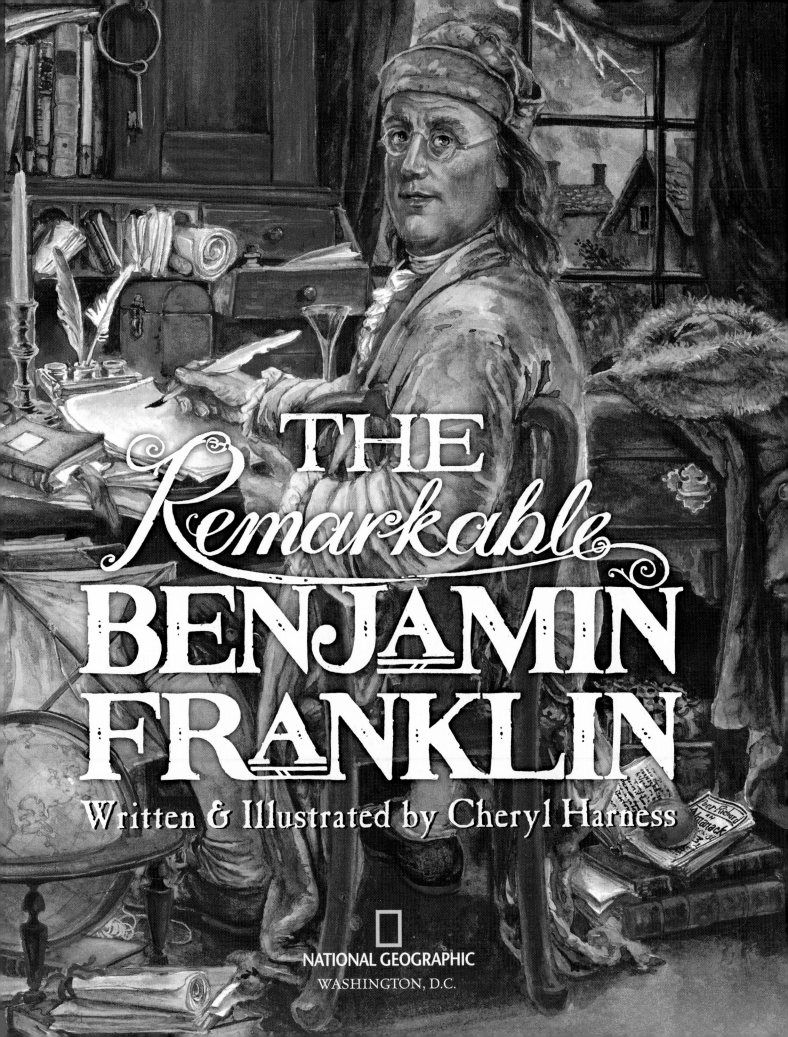

THE *Remarkable* BENJAMIN FRANKLIN

Written & Illustrated by Cheryl Harness

NATIONAL GEOGRAPHIC

WASHINGTON, D.C.

"If you would not be forgotten,

As soon as you are dead and rotten,

Either write things worthy reading,

Or do things worth the writing." B.F.

Eripuit Coelum Fulmen Septrumque Tyrannis.
("He snatched the lighting from heaven and the scepter from tyrants.")
A. R. J. TURGOT

A NOTE FROM THE AUTHOR

In the spring of 1790, twenty thousand people came to Benjamin Franklin's funeral in Philadelphia. Today, visitors to his grave may not even realize how long-gone Mr. Franklin has touched their modern lives. Perhaps they've warmed themselves by a Franklin stove, perhaps been helped by local firemen, and gone to the post office or to the public library (topped with lightning rods) to check out his *Autobiography*, the first masterpiece of American literature. Or they may have read, through their Franklin-invented bifocals, his best-seller, *The Way to Wealth* (in print since 1758). If so—and even if not—they may well have money engraved with Benjamin's picture folded in their pockets. And, as folks have for more than 250 years, they might have peppered their conversations with bits of "Poor Richard's" wisdom.

A few blocks away from his resting place is Independence Hall, where he signed the Declaration of Independence and where later, after working in Europe on the treaty that brought the Revolutionary War to its official end, Benjamin pitched in at the creation of the new nation's Constitution. No other Founding Father signed all of these critical documents.

His life was more than two-thirds gone when he had to give up his valued notion of himself as a Briton. It is as a great American that we remember him because he symbolizes so well the ideals of our republic. People around the world, even those who despise the actions of our government, cling to that American dream: the notion of a place where you can live and think freely; where you might strive to better yourself and be of use to those around you; where you might try to be like Benjamin Franklin.

When Boston folks walked past Josiah Franklin's shop, they wrinkled their noses. Inside, Josiah was turning smelly beef tallow and sheep fat into soap and sleek candles. When people passed by early one winter morning in 1706, they smiled. Sounds from a window over the shuttered shop told them that Abiah, the candlemaker's wife, had a new baby.

Devout Josiah, who devoted a tenth of all he had to God, cradled his tenth son in his arms. Surely this child would be a preacher! Surely this child, youngest son of a youngest son for five generations, was special! The proud father bundled up his new baby and hurried across snowy Milk Street to the Old South Church, where Josiah and Abiah's little son was christened Benjamin.

January 17, 1706

Benjamin's birthday, according to the reformed calendar, in use since 1752

I was put to the grammar school at eight years of age, my father intending to devote me, as a tithe of his sons, to the service of the Church.

—B. F.'s Autobiography

Not long after book-loving Benjamin began school, his dad faced facts. A working man with a big family couldn't pay for a preacher's education. Benjamin's formal schooling came to an early end—but not his learning. That's the great thing to remember about Benjamin.

He helped out at the kettles, vats, and candle molds, but Benjamin preferred reading. And he loved to fish or watch the tall ships in the salty water around his seaport town. He loved the water so much that he taught himself how to do what hardly anyone in his time ever did: swim! He made wooden flippers for his hands and attached himself to a kite so he could swim like a speedy, sturdy, brown-haired fish. That's another thing to know about Benjamin: He really was special.

Josiah saw how smart and curious his boy was, and he knew a sick-of-soap-and-candles, sea-hankering boy when he saw one. He began searching for a trade that would satisfy his restless youngest boy.

The Doors of Wisdom are never shut.
—POOR RICHARD'S ALMANACK (P. R. A.), 1755

1. The typesetter set backward metal letters into a tray called a composing stick. He had to be clever and nimble-fingered. Benjamin was.

The top of the wooden frame folded down over the paper.

paper

tympan

4. While the beater inked the type, the puller (he would pull the press's lever) placed a fresh sheet of paper on the tympan.

These boards attached to the ceiling held the press steady.

2. The columns of type were fitted into an iron frame, which was placed on the bed of the press.

The folded frame was then folded down on to the type.

3. The beater used wood and leather balls to put ink, made of soot and varnish, on the type.

lever

platen

Josiah and his boy met with James Franklin, one of Benjamin's brothers, and made an agreement. In return for ten pounds and nine years of work (forever, it seemed to 12-year-old Benjamin), James would give him his keep and teach him an important trade. In a pre-radio, no-television world in which words on paper were everything, Benjamin would be a printer.

He soon made one of the happiest discoveries any person can make: He and his work were a perfect fit.

He that has a Trade, has an Office of Profit and Honour.
P. R. A., 1756

6

5. Paper and type were slid under the platen, then firmly mashed together when the puller worked the press. A printer did all of these things.

He had to be strong and fast.

Benjamin was.

Printing with moveable type was invented in China, in the 11th century. The printing press came along in Germany in the 1400s. The printed word put words, ideas, and power into the hands of readers, readers such as one determined colonial teenager. That's what Benjamin was.

Before and after work, Benjamin read books. They fed his appetite for learning as well as his new plan: A printer could publish his own ideas. If they were good and well written, people would read them, then reader and writer would have better lives. The young writer-in-training studied the latest London magazines, determined to make his work equally excellent. He copied and cut apart the sentences, rearranged them, and wrote the idea behind each one. Soon Benjamin was eager to show off what he was learning.

...Writing has been of great use to me in the course of my life, and was the principal means of my advancement.

B. F.'s AUTOBIOGRAPHY

On April 2, 1722, the readers of James's newspaper read a letter written by someone calling herself Mrs. Silence Dogood. As soon as they appeared under his front door, James printed the mystery woman's witty letters about such things as her husband's death, schooling for girls, and fashion. Who was this wise lady? The editor's smart-aleck kid brother, that's who. James was furious.

Benjamin, a smart dog on a short leash, wanted to get away from his bossy brother. He sold some of his precious books for traveling money, and one September night the runaway apprentice slipped aboard a southbound sloop. Benjamin looked at the steepled hills of Boston. Somewhere in the darkness were his family and every familiar thing, there on the shrinking shore.

...I liv'd a chearful Country Life, spending my leisure Time either in some innocent Diversion with the neighbouring Females, or in some shady Retirement, with the best of Company, Books....
—Mrs. Silence Dogood, April 2, 1722

Hide not your talents, they for use were made.
What's a sun-dial in the shade! —P. R. A., 1750

·October 6, 1723·

There was no work in the smaller town of New York, so he journeyed on. After a rainy week of hard walking, 17-year-old Benjamin awoke to the sound of church bells. The rising sun shone on a cold, tired, smelly, grimy, hollow-bellied boy just outside of the city of Philadelphia. He followed his nose to a bakery, where he bought three pennies' worth of breakfast. He stuffed a yeasty roll under each arm and, as he walked up Market Street, crammed a third bun into his mouth. A round-faced girl standing in her doorway couldn't help laughing at him.

...I knew no soul nor where to look for lodging. I was fatigued with traveling....

—B. F.'s AUTOBIOGRAPHY

Once he got cleaned up, Benjamin impressed other people, too. Mr. Keimer, a long-bearded printer, gave him a job, Mr. Read, the father of the merry girl, rented him a room, and the girl, Deborah, became his friend. And Pennsylvania's governor gave Benjamin an astounding offer to do the colony's printing—that is, if Benjamin had his own shop. Might his father help set him up in business? Benjamin hurried off to Boston to find out. Old Josiah was impressed with his boy but—a teenager running a print shop? No. Work and save. That was Josiah's good advice. Back Benjamin went to Philadelphia, to his job with Mr. Keimer.

Now the governor had another idea: What if *he* helped Benjamin go to England to choose and buy the necessary equipment? Dazzled Benjamin was bursting to show what he could do if only he had the chance and the money. The governor was promising both! As soon as Benjamin survived the dangerous voyages and had his own shop, he and Debbie Read would marry. They promised each other. A vessel would sail in the fall, and he would be on it. Benjamin promised himself that.

Diligence is the mother of good luck.
—THE WAY TO WEALTH, 1758

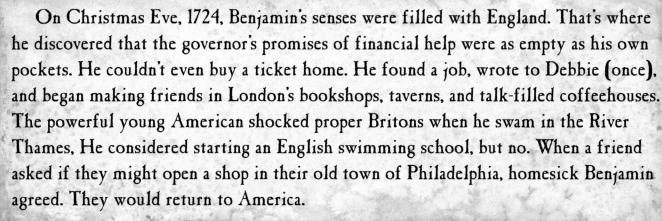

On Christmas Eve, 1724, Benjamin's senses were filled with England. That's where he discovered that the governor's promises of financial help were as empty as his own pockets. He couldn't even buy a ticket home. He found a job, wrote to Debbie (once), and began making friends in London's bookshops, taverns, and talk-filled coffeehouses. The powerful young American shocked proper Britons when he swam in the River Thames. He considered starting an English swimming school, but no. When a friend asked if they might open a shop in their old town of Philadelphia, homesick Benjamin agreed. They would return to America.

Blessed is he that expects nothing, for he shall never be disappointed.
—P. R. A., 1739

On his way west in the summer of 1726, Benjamin recorded in his journal his seaweed experiments and the sight of an eerie night rainbow arching over the moonlit Atlantic. With a thermometer on a rope, he took the ocean's temperature and became the first scientist to measure what he called the Gulf Stream. It was a great current of warm water that flowed through the cold sea. And Benjamin wrote down new plans for his time, his thoughts, and his money. As soon as the boat landed, a fresh, a better chapter of his life would begin. He couldn't wait.

Those who write of the art of poetry teach us that if we would write what may be worth the reading, we ought always, before we begin, to form a regular plan and design....I am apt to think it is the same as to life.
—B. F.'s Journal, 1726

The colonial governor avoided him. Debbie had married someone else. And soon, after his shopkeeping partner got sick and died, Benjamin was back working at Mr. Keimer's press, all the more determined to put his plans to work.

He started a club for working men like himself, who wanted to improve themselves, their businesses, and their city. The members of the Junto would talk and write about books and philosophical ideas. Could a person, for instance, make himself perfect? Benjamin tried to. He listed goodness goals (13 "Virtues") and tracked his daily progress. He never accomplished perfection but—professional independence? A family of his own? He did win those things.

I wished to live without committing any fault at any time.
—B. F.'s AUTOBIOGRAPHY

1. TEMPERANCE   4. RESOLUTION   7. SINCERITY   10. CLEANLINESS
2. SILENCE   5. FRUGALITY   8. JUSTICE   11. TRANQUILITY
3. ORDER   6. INDUSTRY   9. MODERATION   12. CHASTITY
13. HUMILITY

By practicing his Virtues—especially Industry (working hard) and Frugality (saving money)—and with luck and a Junto friend's help, 24-year-old Benjamin did at last, in July 1730, become the owner of his own print shop and editor of his own newspaper. Less than two months later, he mended an old, broken promise when he and Deborah Read, whose mean, rascally first husband had left the country, revived their old affection for each other. They set up housekeeping and became good partners in their printing and stationery business and in their family, which included Debbie's mother and Benjamin's infant son, William. Who was William's mother? That has been a mystery for nearly 300 years.

A good Wife and Health, is a Man's best Wealth.
—P. R. A., 1746

In his paper, the *Pennsylvania Gazette*, Benjamin printed ideas (well discussed in the Junto) that set Philadelphians to dreaming of what their city could have if they put their heads, hands, and money together. A library. Volunteer firefighters. Paved and lighted streets. A hospital. All of these civic notions and more were born in the busy brain of citizen Benjamin Franklin.

Three months after Debbie had their son Francis, in the fall of 1732, the *Gazette* announced another new arrival: *Poor Richard's Almanack*. Folks still repeat "Richard's" (Benjamin's) sensible sayings from this information-stuffed best-seller. Its author's life was every bit as loaded with things that interested him: his clubs, his printing and writing, his part-time jobs (colonial assembly clerk and town postmaster), his books, and most of all, his family—his two much-loved boys. Benjamin could hardly stand it when he lost them. Smallpox killed four-year-old Franky, and, years later, a revolution would rob him of William.

Our articles of agreement obliged every member to keep always in good order and fit for use, a certain number of leather buckets...which were to be brought to every fire.... —B. F.'s Autobiography

Because heat from Benjamin's Pennsylvania Fireplace goes out into the room instead of up the chimney, folks who have a "Franklin Stove" don't have to use as much firewood to keep warm.

HEAT radiates.

HEAT circulates.

SMOKE goes up the chimney.

COLD AIR comes in from the cellar.

Years of hard work bought Benjamin more time to play with his new daughter, Sally, born in 1743. He tinkered with new ideas, such as a better way to heat homes. If he had patented his popular "Franklin Stove," he'd have been richer by far, but money wasn't as important to Benjamin as understanding life and making it better for people. Besides, his curiosity was lit up with a fire much more interesting than the one on his hearth.

The noblest question in the World is What Good may I do in it?
—P. R. A., 1737

Benjamin in his wig

Electricity-generating device. Soon Benjamin will invent his own "electrostatic machine."

Glass rod charged with static electricity

A "Leyden jar" was part of Benjamin's electrical equipment. It could "hold" and discharge electricity. The bigger the jar, the bigger the spark, which could electrocute a fly or a chicken or impress the neighbors.

On a trip to Boston, Benjamin saw a man make "electrical fire." A boy's hair stood on end, and crackling sparks flew from his fingertips! Amazed, Benjamin bought the man's equipment. He sent for the latest information from Europe, where electrical demonstrations were delighting all sorts of people. He had to learn everything he could about this mysterious force.

I had secured leisure during the rest of my life for philosophical studies and amusements. I purchased all Dr. Spence's apparatus...and I proceeded in my electrical experiments with great alacrity.

—B. F.'s AUTOBIOGRAPHY

What was it that could—and did!—shock him clear off his feet? And were there, as some thought, two, opposing and attracting, kinds of electricity? No. Benjamin's great discovery, that electricity could be both "positive" and "negative," was published in London, in 1751. Then, on a stormy June day in 1752, with a key and a kite, Benjamin answered another question: Were lightning and electricity really, scientifically, the same thing?

Yes!

The experiment, which could have killed him, brought worldwide fame and honorary college degrees to "Dr. Franklin," the man who'd captured lightning in a bottle. What did he do with his discovery? He invented something not only useful but lifesaving: "lightning rods." Atop buildings, they directed thunderbolts that might otherwise set rooftops on fire, down a wire and into the Earth.

Experiments made in electricity first gave philosophers a suspicion that the matter of lightning was the same with the electric matter.
—B. F.'s ESSAY, SEPTEMBER 1767

The quarrels of greedy European kings were spilling over into the land beyond the American Colonies. In wild western Pennsylvania, settlers were being attacked by French raiders and their Indian allies. Benjamin's town was in real danger so, when the colonial rulers wouldn't, he organized a militia and trained alongside his neighbors. When the fighting stopped, Pennsylvanians elected him to the colonial legislature.

Three years later, in 1754, when the worst of the French and Indian wars began in earnest, Benjamin met with other colonial delegates and tribesmen from the Six Nations to plan their fight against France. He wondered: If town folks could defend themselves, if native tribes could unite, why not the Colonies? He illustrated his idea (the first official plan for a united America) with a drawing of a snake cut into colonial chunks. "JOIN, or DIE," said the caption on America's first political cartoon. His plan might well have kept the Revolutionary War from ever happening, but it was ahead of its time. The 13 Colonies didn't trust each other. Their king, George II, over in England, didn't trust the Colonies. He did, however, send an army to defend them.

JOIN, or DIE

—PENNSYLVANIA GAZETTE, MAY 9, 1754

Benjamin was asked to set aside his efforts to win the war against France. He needed to go to England and pay a visit to the descendants of the colony's founder, William Penn. They owned vast acres of Pennsylvania, yet they refused to pay any taxes to the cash-poor colony. Since Debbie would not risk Sally's life or her own by crossing the deep, cold, stormy ocean, only their slaves, Peter and King, sailed away with the Franklins, father and son. (Many years would pass before Benjamin worked to end the sorry, evil practice of slavery.)

Who is strong? He that can conquer his bad Habits.
— P. R. A., 1744

In July 1757, 51-year-old Benjamin, former stranded teenager, was a great scientist and unofficial colonial ambassador. His longtime pen pals introduced him to worldly people who shared his love of talk and good books. He visited other parts of Europe, but Benjamin loved London, the foggy center of the 18th century's superpower. He was proud of his English heritage and of America, where a person had a fairer chance to improve himself, as he had done. Most Londoners were poor, stuck in hard lives occasionally brightened by fairs, preachers, puppet shows, cockfights, and glimpses of rich folks, such as the famous Dr. Franklin. The aristocrats in Britain's government, however, did not care how well known, well dressed, and stylishly wigged Benjamin might be. They did not intend to be charmed by a commoner from wild America. It was only after a long legal wrangle that Benjamin wrestled a compromise from the snobbish Penn family.

Benjamin sailed home in 1762. By then, England had a new young king, George III, and Benjamin had a grandson, Temple. William, like his own dad, did not marry his son's mother. Eventually, though, by the time Benjamin returned to London in 1764, William did have a bride and a new job: royal governor of New Jersey. And by then, the king and his 13 American Colonies were beginning to get on each other's nerves.

It had cost plenty to drive France out of America, so the British demanded that the Americans, British citizens with no official say in the royal legislature, buy a small tax stamp for all of their necessary papers. More hateful taxes—on tea, among other things—followed. The prideful misunderstandings they caused, on both sides of the Atlantic, poisoned Benjamin's dream of an ocean-divided empire of equals.

I set out immediately, with my son, for London, and we only stopped a little by the way to view Stonehenge on Salisbury Plain.
—B. F.'s AUTOBIOGRAPHY

Dost thou love life? Then do not squander time; for that's the stuff life is made of. —P. R. A., 1746

23

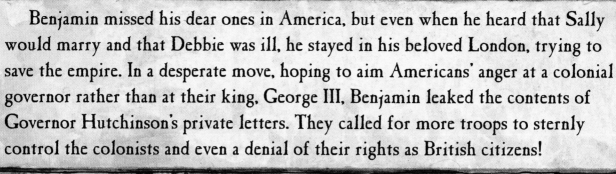

Benjamin missed his dear ones in America, but even when he heard that Sally would marry and that Debbie was ill, he stayed in his beloved London, trying to save the empire. In a desperate move, hoping to aim Americans' anger at a colonial governor rather than at their king, George III, Benjamin leaked the contents of Governor Hutchinson's private letters. They called for more troops to sternly control the colonists and even a denial of their rights as British citizens!

You may shut up their Ports, one by one.... You may reduce their Cities to Ashes; but the Flame of Liberty in North America shall not be extinguished....A great Country of hearty Peasants is not to be subdued. —B. F.'S LETTER TO LORD BUCKINGHAMSHIRE, APRIL 2, 1774

January 29, 1774

The plan backfired. Furious colonists, hearing of the governor's words, tossed taxed tea into Boston Harbor. Just as furious was the king when he heard of Franklin's part in this outrageous turn of events. Benjamin was ordered to appear before the king's ministers. Scandal-mad Londoners came, eager to see an international celebrity brought low, laughed at, and insulted. But if they thought Benjamin felt humiliated or disgraced, then they were fools. Behind his icy stare was silent outrage. His dream of a British empire of equals was at an end. Finally, in the spring of 1775, Benjamin Franklin, American rebel, was on his way home.

Love your enemies, for they will tell you their faults.
—P. R. A., 1756

On April 19, 1775, in Lexington, Massachusetts, the troubles between colonists and British soldiers flared into fighting. The Revolutionary War had begun. Two weeks later, after more than ten years in Europe, Benjamin, along with his teenage grandson, Temple, was welcomed home by Sally, her husband, Mr. Bache, and their children. Benjamin's wife, Deborah, the long-ago laughing girl, had died.

Five days after he stepped off the boat, Benjamin went to the State House to take his place at the Continental Congress. He'd met tall George Washington, but most of the delegates were young strangers. Many of them still hoped for peace with Britain. Not Benjamin. His hurt equaled the love he'd had for the empire, and that went for his son, too. William was stubbornly loyal to Britain. Benjamin cut them both out of his heart.

They that can give up essential liberty to obtain a little temporary safety deserve neither liberty nor safety.
—B.F., HISTORICAL REVIEW OF PENNSYLVANIA, 1759

The delegates in Philadelphia chose Washington to lead the Continental Army and Benjamin to be postmaster. That was easy. Now the penniless Congress had to come up with forces to fight the world's most powerful empire. The patriots captured Montreal but were horribly beaten at Quebec. In June 1775, the British won a bloody victory at Bunker (Breed's) Hill, then occupied nearby Boston. Not until March 1776 were they driven out by George Washington's troops. Meanwhile, the delegates faced a decision.

God helps them that help themselves.
—P. R. A., 1736

If the delegates from the American Colonies voted to break away from Britain, they would have to explain to the people of the world (who generally believed that monarchs were set on their thrones by the will of God) why they were rebelling against their lawful king. Tall, lanky Thomas Jefferson of Virginia drafted the manifesto then took what he had written to Benjamin, the old editor. He sharpened up some of the phrases, then the entire Congress argued over every word. What they were doing was dead serious, historic, radical—words were everything! At last, on July 4, the men voted, and Jefferson took the final version to leather-aproned printers.

You and I were long friends: you are now my enemy,
and I am Yours, B. Franklin
    —B. F.'s UNSENT LETTER TO A BRITISH FRIEND,
                        JULY 5, 1775

At noon on July 8, 1776, people crowded onto the State House yard to listen to a reading of the Declaration of Independence. With these last words, "...we mutually pledge to each other our Lives, our Fortunes and our sacred Honor," there were, no doubt, grim thoughts and tears as well as cheers, 13 cannon blasts, and deep chimes from the bell that would be called Liberty.

It's one thing to write such a document. Imagine signing it and branding yourself a traitorous revolutionary! As the delegates wrote their names, John Hancock of Boston is said to have remarked that the signers must all now hang together. Some said that old Benjamin wisecracked back, "Yes, we must indeed all hang together, or else, most assuredly, we shall all hang separately."

Without freedom of thought there can be no such thing as wisdom;
and no such thing as liberty without freedom of speech.
—Mrs. Silence Dogood, July 9, 1722

In New York, General Washington's soldiers faced a huge fleet of warships full of British troops. Thousands of bayonets glittered like the sharp claws of an angry lion, ready to pounce on a baby eagle. At this critical moment, Benjamin and two of his fellow rebels, John Adams of Massachusetts and Edward Rutledge of South Carolina, journeyed to meet Lord Howe, the king's admiral. In a crowded inn along the way, Benjamin and the stocky Mr. Adams had a legendary argument over the window in their room. Benjamin won: It stayed open. On September 11, 1776, they walked past a living stockade of tall, stern soldiers to meet with the aristocratic officer. He politely offered lunch to his guests and a chance to give up this unfortunate revolution, as British subjects, or fight it—as enemies. The Americans would fight.

Four days later, British forces captured the city of New York. General Washington and his poorly armed soldiers fought and retreated again and again up Manhattan Island. As the year 1776 came to an end, the barely begun revolution was in terrible trouble. The men of the Continental Congress knew that their only hope was across the ocean. Someone had to go to Paris and beg help from their old enemy: France. Without it, America's patriot cause was doomed. Benjamin Franklin began packing.

Early to bed and early to rise, makes a man healthy, wealthy, and wise.
                                                —P. R. A., 1735

No Gains without Pains.
—P. R. A., 1745

Britain was the most powerful empire in the 1700s but, from Ireland to Russia, high-class people envied and admired the culture of France. And whom did the French most admire? The great scientist who'd stolen sacred fire from the heavens, then stood up to hated England! The witty Bonhomme Richard of the *Almanack*. To himself, he was a tired-out old man on a mission. He and his two grandsons, Benny Bache and Temple, had just survived a cold voyage across stormy seas afloat with men eager to put a famous traitor in chains. On December 21, 1776, as General Washington's ragged army shivered 3,000 miles away, cheering Parisians surrounded the carriage of fur-hatted Dr. Franklin, superstar.

What you would seem to be, be really.
—P. R. A., 1744

Privately, stealthily, America got money and weapons but no official help from France. King Louis XVI had no love for revolutions—except for one that would sting his enemy: Britain. But did he wish to anger it by helping rebellious losers? *Non.* A desperately needed military pact with France could be earned only by a big American victory. It happened at last, in October 1777, when about 5,000 redcoats were captured at Saratoga, New York. On February 6, 1778, the vital treaty was signed. Benjamin, wearing the coat he'd worn in London in 1774, on the day of insults, watched with grim satisfaction. Now, shy, tubby Louis XVI and his fancy queen, Marie Antoinette, could officially meet the representatives of revolutionary America. Now, Benjamin knew, the defeat of Britain was possible. American independence was possible.

There is no little enemy.
  —P. R. A., 1733

The lady is playing an ARMONICA, Benjamin's invention. Her moistened fingers on the revolving glasses make soft, delicate music.

When he was young, Benjamin made sure that his Philadelphia neighbors saw how hard-working and thrifty he truly was because they valued those qualities and he needed their business. Now, when his country badly needed the approval of pleasure-loving French aristocrats, he pleased them with an easy going version of himself. Their artificial society was old and rule-bound. To them he was the wigless, bespectacled philosopher from a young, idealistic country: a simple man. Ha! Benjamin was anything but!

Eat to please thyself, but dress to please others.
—P. R. A., 1738

With little French-speaking ability, he fought for America's independence.
His weapons: charm and wily intelligence. His battlefields: his messy desk, a small
printing press, and candlelit parlors. He laid the groundwork for much needed loans
and trade. To get and make gunpowder, he worked with the great chemist Antoine-
Laurent Lavoisier. He helped would-be warriors such as Baron von Steuben and the
teenage Marquis de Lafayette to join the fight in America. Artists, scientists,
Americans needing help, flirtatious ladies, all came to visit Benjamin.

*Human felicity is produced not so much by great pieces of good
fortune that seldom happen, as by little advantages that occur every day.*
—B. F.'s AUTOBIOGRAPHY

At last, in 1781, the bloody, cruel war ground to an end, and the Americans, with the help of the French Navy at Yorktown, won their independence from Great Britain. In Paris, Benjamin, John Adams, and John Jay labored over the complicated peace and trade agreements until, at last, on September 3, 1783, the final, formal treaty was signed, and the United States was born.

When, in the summer of 1785, it came time for Benjamin to leave, a carriage was too bumpy and painful for a sore-jointed old man. Queen Marie Antoinette loaned him her litter and two gentle mules for his farewell journey to France's coast. In England, he saw old friends and William, his loyalist-in-exile son, one last time, then he and his tall-grown grandsons sailed west to the nation that Benjamin had helped to invent.

There never was a good war or a bad peace.
—B. F.'s LETTER TO JOSIAH QUINCY,
SEPTEMBER 11, 1783

September 14, 1785

What a chiming, ding-donging, gun-booming, cheering welcome awaited 79-year-old Benjamin when he got home! And, not long after, a new job: president of the state of Pennsylvania (much like being a modern-day governor). But, as always, he made time for what stirred his busy brain and his heart. New grandchildren. Building projects, such as a print shop for his grandson, Benny Bache. Making English easier to spell. Inventions, such as an arm extender for reaching books from the tall shelves in the library he had built on to his house. A "rolling press" for copying the many letters he wrote as he soaked his naked old self in cool morning air or in his copper tub. He met with other curious men at the American Philosophical Society. He was president of it, too, and of the nation's first anti-slavery society. Again, Benjamin was far, far ahead of his time.

We landed at Market Street wharf, where we were received by a crowd of people with huzzahs, and accompanied with acclamations quite to my door. Found my family well. God be praised and thanked for all his mercies!
—B. F.'S LETTER TO DAVID HARTLEY, SEPTEMBER 11, 1785

It's one thing to win a war. It's another for a new nation to run itself and pay its bills. Could the United States do it? So far, not very well. Everyone agreed that something must be done. In the spring of 1787, a call went out to the states for men to come back to Philadelphia.

PENNSYLVANIA STATE HOUSE

In this world nothing can be said to be certain, except death and taxes.
— B. F.'s LETTER TO JEAN BAPTISTE LE ROY,
NOVEMBER 13, 1789

Four sturdy men carried Benjamin, in his sedan chair, back to the State House, where he joined the men sitting around the familiar tables. George Washington, chosen to preside, walked to the front of the room and sat down on a tall, curvy chair into which a sun was carved, peeking over a polished horizon. Sentries guarded the door, and James Madison of Virginia began recording the secret sessions of the Constitutional Convention. Hard enough it would be to thrash out all of the delegates' ideas about what kind of nation theirs should be without outsiders chiming in. It would take a miracle, everyone agreed, to come up with a government that would work for their time and for the unimaginable years to come.

We were sent here to consult, not to contend with each other.
—B. F. IN THE RECORD OF THE
CONSTITUTIONAL CONVENTION

There would be a judicial branch, topped by a Supreme Court, and an executive branch, topped by a man elected for a short time so he wouldn't be too kingly. As the weather warmed, hot arguments over the legislative branch about killed the convention. Big and small states had to be equally represented—but how? The delegates compromised: A House of Representatives, elected according to population, and a Senate, with two people from each state. All of this and plenty more obsessed the men that summer. Difficult subjects, such as slavery, were put off. Many people were frightened that a too-powerful government would squash the liberties of individual citizens and states. (Had they gotten out from under a king only to be bossed by homegrown politicians?) A Bill of Rights, added later, would fix the problem.

I wish the bald eagle had not been chosen as the representative of our country; he is a bird of bad moral character....The turkey...is a much more respectable bird, and withal a true original native of America.
                                                    —B. F.'s letter to Sally Bache,
                                                                January 26, 1784

September 17, 1787

The new government would work, Benjamin figured, as long as the people in it ran it well. As long as the citizens were good and strong, their government would be, too. The delegates took Benjamin's advice and agreed to accept the new laws "unanimously." As they signed the Constitution, he gazed at the carved sun on the tall, curvy chair. At last, he had "the happiness to know that it is a rising and not a setting sun."

In Philadelphia today, in Independence Hall, that wooden sun on Washington's chair still has not risen or set. Citizens still argue. The miraculous United States Constitution is an ongoing experiment, a work in progress.

I agree to this Constitution with all its faults.
—B. F. IN THE RECORD OF THE CONSTITUTIONAL CONVENTION,
SEPTEMBER 17, 1787

Benjamin spent his remaining time on Earth pondering things that still made him curious. Had the Earth always been magnetic? How did fossils of warm-weather animals come to be found in cold places? Had the Poles shifted? Would the world keep getting better? News of revolution in his much loved France troubled him. So did Americans' treatment of the Indians and the Congress's refusal to end slavery. "Mankind," Benjamin believed, "was equally designed for the enjoyment of happiness."

Slavery is such an atrocious debasement of human nature....
—B. F.'s Address to the Public, from the Pennsylvania Society for Promoting the Abolition of Slavery, November 9, 1789

He was happy, in spite of his painful, 84-year-old body. He was content with his family, pleased to have lived to see the "grand machine" of America's government begin to work, and delighted that his friend George Washington was its first President. Benjamin's daughter and grandchildren were nearby when he slipped out of his 18th-century world.

April 17, 1790

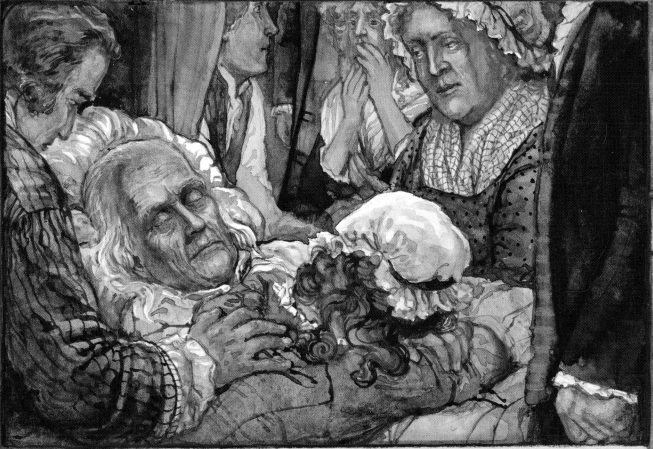

Benjamin Franklin was, indeed, very special, just as his father, Josiah, had known from the very beginning.

The Body of B Franklin Printer (like the cover of an old book, its contents torn out and stripped of its lettering and gilding) lies here, food for worms. But the work shall not be lost; for it will, (as he believed) appear once more, in a new and more elegant edition, revised and corrected, by the Author. B. F., EPITAPH, 1728

The 18th-Century World of Benjamin Franklin

1706 January 17: Benjamin Franklin is born in Boston, Massachusetts Bay Colony, 15th of his parents' 17 children.

1707 The kingdoms of England, Wales, and Scotland unite to form Great Britain.

1716 Benjamin leaves school to work in his father's shop.

1718 Benjamin starts learning the printer's trade.
November 21: Edward Teach, aka the ferocious pirate Blackbeard, is captured.

1719 Daniel Defoe writes *Robinson Crusoe* based on a true story.

1721 Johann Sebastian Bach writes the Brandenburg Concertos.

1723 Benjamin runs away from home. He ends up in Philadelphia, Pennsylvania.

1724–1726 Benjamin lives and works in London.

1726 Jonathan Swift publishes his book *Gulliver's Travels*.

1727 Back in Philadelphia, Benjamin invents a community-action network: the Junto.

1729 He begins publishing and editing the *Pennsylvania Gazette*.

1730 September 1: Benjamin Franklin marries Deborah Read Rogers. About this same time Benjamin's son William is born.

1731 Benjamin's Junto establishes America's first circulating library.
Benjamin Banneker, black American mathematician/astronomer, is born in Maryland.

1732 February 22: George Washington, 1st U.S. President, is born in Virginia.
March 31: Joseph Hayden, Austrian composer, is born.
October 20: Benjamin's son Francis Folger Franklin is born.
December: First edition of *Poor Richard's Almanack* is published.

1734 November 2: Daniel Boone, trailblazer, is born in Pennsylvania.

1735 January 1: Paul Revere, American patriot, is born in Massachusetts.
October 30: John Adams, 2nd U.S. President, is born there, too.

1736 Benjamin starts the Union Fire Company in Philadelphia.
November 21: His four-year-old son Francis dies.

1737 Benjamin becomes Philadelphia's postmaster.

ADAMS

WASHINGTON

1738   June 4: The future King George III is born in London, England.

1740   Maria Theresa of Austria is crowned Holy Roman Empress.

1741   George Friedrich Handel composes *Messiah*.
Benjamin is developing his Pennsylvania Fireplace, aka the "Franklin Stove."

1742   Anders Celsius of Switzerland invents the centigrade thermometer.

1743   April 13: Thomas Jefferson, 3rd U.S. President, is born in Virginia.
**September 11: Sarah "Sally" Franklin is born.
Benjamin begins the American Philosophical Society, a club for scientists, to promote "useful knowledge."**

1748   **September: Benjamin retires from the printing business so he can spend more time on scientific experiments and his community.**
Discovered in Italy: ruins of Pompeii, destroyed by volcano in AD 79

1749   **Benjamin proposes a school: the Academy of Pennsylvania. In time, it will become the University of Pennsylvania.**

1751   March 16: James Madison, 4th U.S. President, is born in Virginia.
Benjamin invents a kind of fund raising still in use today: Money, collected by the people, is matched by the government. In this way, he gets America's first city hospital built.

1752   January 1: Legendary flagmaker Betsy Ross is born in Pennsylvania.
June: Benjamin's electrical experiment with the kite and the key. For his scientific achievements, he is awarded the Copley Medal, the 18th-century version of today's Nobel Prize. He will use his discovery to invent the lightning rod.
September 14: The British Empire adopts the more accurate Gregorian calendar.
Benjamin's birthday, January 6, on the old Julian calendar, becomes January 17.

1753   Carolus Linnaeus of Sweden establishes the scientific method of naming plants and animals.
August 10: Benjamin becomes Deputy Postmaster General for the northern colonies.

1754   French and Indian War begins near present-day Pittsburgh, Pennsylvania.
Benjamin develops a plan that would unite the Colonies.

1755   November 2: Marie Antoinette, future queen of France, is born in Austria.

1756   January 2: Composer Wolfgang Amadeus Mozart is born in Austria.

1757   **The Pennsylvania Assembly sends Benjamin to England.**

1758   April 28: James Monroe, 5th U.S. President, is born in Virginia.
Benjamin publishes *The Way to Wealth*.

1761 September 22: Coronation of 23-year-old King George III

1762 Catherine the Great becomes empress of Russia.
Benjamin returns to Philadelphia. He brings along his new invention: the glass armonica.

1764 St. Louis, first permanent French settlement on the Mississippi is founded.
November: Benjamin sails again to London.

1765 British Parliament passes the Stamp Act as a means of taxing Americans.

1767 March 15: Andrew Jackson, 7th U.S. President, is born in one of the Carolinas (no one knows which one).
July 11: John Quincy Adams, 6th U.S. President, is born in Massachusetts.

1769 First lightning rods are placed on rooftops.
July 16: Father Junipero Serra founds the first California mission at San Diego.
August 15: Napoleon Bonaparte, future emperor of France, is born in Corsica.
Pontiac, warrior and unifying tribal leader, dies in Cahokia, Illinois.

1770 March 5: Violence breaks out between British troops and Americans in Boston.
August 1: William Clark, explorer, is born in Virginia.
December 16: Composer Ludwig van Beethoven is born in Germany.
Explorer James Bruce discovers the source of the Blue Nile River in Africa.

1771 **Benjamin begins writing his *Autobiography*.**

1773 February 9: William Henry Harrison, 9th U.S. President, is born in Virginia.
December 16: Tax protest known as the Boston Tea Party takes place.

1774 Mother Ann Lee and a band of followers, to be known as the Shakers, land in America.
August 18: Meriwether Lewis, explorer, is born in Virginia.
September 5: The First Continental Congress convenes in Philadelphia.
December 19: Deborah Read Franklin, age 66, dies.

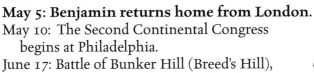

1775 April 19: First shots of the Revolutionary War are fired at Lexington and Concord, Massachusetts.
May 5: Benjamin returns home from London.
May 10: The Second Continental Congress begins at Philadelphia.
June 17: Battle of Bunker Hill (Breed's Hill), near Boston, Massachusetts, is fought.
July 3: General George Washington takes command of the Continental Army.
December 16: Jane Austen, great English novelist, is born.
Daniel Boone makes the Wilderness Road to Kentucky.

> Throughout the 1700s inventions such as the spinning jenny and James Watt's improved engine are making possible a turning point in history:
>
> THE INDUSTRIAL REVOLUTION.

1776 January 9: Thomas Paine publishes his patriotic best-seller: *Common Sense*.
July 4: The Declaration of Independence is adopted.
October 27: Benjamin Franklin sails to Paris.
December 25–26: General Washington and his men cross the Delaware River
    into New Jersey. Their victory there saves the failing American Revolution.

1777 October 17: Turning point in the war: American victory at Saratoga, New York.

1778 February 6: The United States and France become partners against the British.
James Cook discovers the Hawaiian Islands.

1781 October 19: British forces surrender to General Washington at Yorktown, Virginia.
British Astronomer William Herschel discovers the planet Uranus.

1783 September 3: Treaty of Paris formally ends the Revolutionary War for American independence.
**December 1: In Paris, Benjamin witnesses the Montgolfier brothers' first manned flights
    in lighter-than-air balloons.**

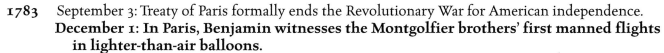

1784 **Benjamin invents bifocals so he can see near and far through
    the same glasses.**
December 5: Phillis Wheatley, black American poet, dies in Boston.
Great Britain takes political control of India.

1785 January 7: Jean-Pierre Blanchard and Dr. John Jeffries cross the English Channel in a hot-air balloon.
    In 1793, Dr. Jeffries will make the first balloon voyage in the United States.
September 14: Benjamin returns home to Philadelphia.

1787 January 27–February 4: Shays's Rebellion, a tax revolt in Massachusetts, tests the strength of the
    new American government.
**May 25–September 17: Benjamin is a delegate to the United States Constitutional
    Convention in Philadelphia.**
February 23: Emma Hart Willard, champion of higher education for girls, is born in Connecticut.
August 22: Inventor John Fitch launches his steamboat on the Delaware River.

1788 June 21: The U.S. Constitution goes into effect.

Benjamin
FRANKLIN

1789 Antoine-Laurent Lavoisier publishes the first modern chemistry textbook.
April 28: Mutiny at sea on the HMS *Bounty*.
April 30: George Washington's Inauguration Day in New York City.
July 14: Parisians storm the Bastille prison. The French
    Revolution begins.

1790 March 29: John Tyler, 10th U.S. President, is born in Virginia.
April 17: Benjamin Franklin dies in Philadelphia.
July 16: George Washington signs legislation establishing
    the first permanent federal city in what is
    now known as Washington, D.C.
August 10: The *Columbia* is the first American
    vessel to sail around the world.

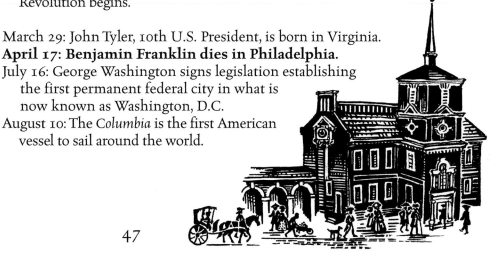

Key to the painting on pages 40–41

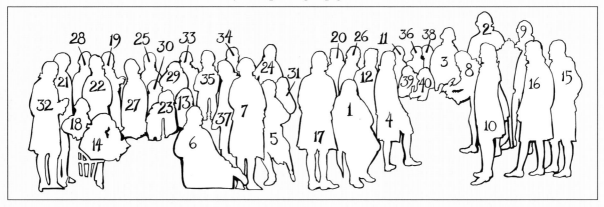

1. Benjamin Franklin (Pa.), 2. George Washington (Va.), 3. James Madison (Va.), 4. Alexander Hamilton (N.Y.), 5. Gouverneur Morris (Pa.), 6. Robert Morris (Pa.), 7. James Wilson (Pa.), 8. Charles C. Pinckney (S.C.), 9. Charles Pinckney (S.C.), 10. John Rutledge (S.C.), 11. Pierce Butler (S.C.), 12. Roger Sherman (Conn.), 13. William S. Johnson (Conn.), 14. James McHenry (Md.), 15. George Read (Del.), 16. Richard Bassett, (Del.), 17. Richard D. Spaight (N.C.), 18. William Blount (N.C.), 19. Hugh Williamson (N.C.), 20. Daniel Jenifer (Md.), 21. Rufus King (Mass.), 22. Nathaniel Gorham (Mass.), 23. Jonathan Dayton (N.J.), 24. Daniel Carroll (Md.), 25. William Few (Ga.), 26. Abraham Baldwin (Ga.), 27. John Langdon (N.H.), 28. Nicholas Gilman (N.H.), 29. William Livingston (N.J.), 30. William Paterson (N.J.), 31. Thomas Mifflin (Pa.), 32. George Clymer (Pa.), 33. Thomas Fitzsimmons (Pa.), 34. Jared Ingersoll (Pa.), 35. Gunning Bedford, Jr. (Del.), 36. Jacob Broom (Del.), 37. John Dickinson (Del.), 38. John Blair (Va.), 39. David Brearley (N.J.), 40. William Jackson (S.C.), secretary.

If you are planning a visit to Benjamin Franklin's city, the best places to start are:

Independence National Historical Park
313 Walnut Street
Philadelphia, Pa. 19106
tel.: 215.597.8974
www.nps.gov/inde/franklin-court

The Franklin Institute
222 N. 20th Street
Philadelphia, Pa. 19103
tel.: 215.448.1200
http://sln.fi.edu/franklin/

NOTE ABOUT QUOTES

Benjamin Franklin's writings are published in many fine collections. The quotes I used for this book are from Dr. Franklin's *The Autobiography and Other Writings*, Peter Shaw, Editor [Bantam Books, 1982] and *The Papers of Benjamin Franklin* (36 volumes so far), edited by Leonard Larabee et.al., Yale University.

BIBLIOGRAPHY

* indicates a book especially recommended for young readers
*Adler, David A. *B. Franklin, Printer.* New York: Holiday House, 2001; Brands, H. W. *The First American.* New York: Doubleday, 2000; Burlingame, Roger. *Benjamin Franklin: Envoy Extraordinary.* New York: Coward-McCann, Inc., 1967; *Fleming, Candace. *Ben Franklin's Almanac.* New York: Atheneum, 2003; Franklin, Benjamin. *The Autobiography.* New York: Bantam Classic Edition, 1982; *Fritz, Jean. *What's the Big Idea, Ben Franklin?* New York: Putnam, 1976; *Giblin, James Cross. *The Amazing Life of Benjamin Franklin.* New York: Scholastic Press, 2000; Isaacson, Walter. *Benjamin Franklin.* New York: Simon & Schuster, 2003; Larabee, Leonard W., Ed. *The Papers of Benjamin Franklin.* New Haven, Conn.: Yale University Press, 1966; *Looby, Chris. *Benjamin Franklin.* New York: Chelsea House Publishers, 1990; Lopez, Claude-Anne. *Mon Cher Papa.* New Haven, Conn.: Yale University Press, 1966; *Mara, Wil. *Benjamin Franklin.* New York: Children's Press, 2002; *Monjo, F. N. *Poor Richard in France.* New York: Holt, Rinehart and Winston, 1973; Morgan, Edmund S. *Benjamin Franklin.* New Haven, Conn.: Yale University Press, 2002; Potter, Robert R. *Benjamin Franklin.* New York: Silver Burdett Press, Inc., 1991; *Randolph, Ryan P. *Benjamin Franklin.* New York: Rosen Publishing Group, 2003; *Scarf, Maggi. *Meet Benjamin Franklin.* New York: Step-Up Books, 1968.

Library of Congress Cataloging-in-Publication Data

Harness, Cheryl.
The remarkable Benjamin Franklin / written and illustrated by Cheryl Harness.
p. cm.
Includes bibliographical references.
Audience: Grades 4–6.
1. Franklin, Benjamin, 1706–1790—Juvenile literature. 2. Statesmen—United States—Biography—Juvenile literature. 3. Scientists—United States—Biography—Juvenile literature. 4. Inventors—United States—Biography—Juvenile literature. 5. Printers—United States—Biography—Juvenile literature. I. Title.
E302.6.F8H315 2005
973.3'092—dc22
2004020504

Printed in the U.S.A.

One of the world's largest nonprofit scientific and educational organizations, the National Geographic Society was founded in 1888 "for the increase and diffusion of geographic knowledge." Fulfilling this mission, the Society educates and inspires millions every day through its magazines, books, television programs, videos, maps and atlases, research grants, the National Geographic Bee, teacher workshops, and innovative classroom materials. The Society is supported through membership dues, charitable gifts, and income from the sale of its educational products. This support is vital to National Geographic's mission to increase global understanding and promote conservation of our planet through exploration, research, and education.

For more information, please call 1-800-NGS LINE (647-5463) or write to the following address:

National Geographic Society
1145 17th Street N.W.
Washington, D.C. 20036-4688 U.S.A.

Visit the Society's Web site at www.nationalgeographic.com.